Gooseberry Patch

chili

Classics

Next to jazz music, there is nothing that lifts
the spirits and strengthens the soul more
than a good bowl of chili.

-Harry James

Rich & Meaty Chili

1 lb. ground beef
1/2 c. onion, chopped
2 15-1/2 oz. cans kidney
    beans
2 15-oz. cans chili beans
6-oz. can tomato paste
4 c. tomatoes, diced
1 c. celery, chopped
1 c. green pepper, chopped

1-1/2 c. water
2 to 3 t. chili powder
1-1/2 t. salt
1/2 t. dried oregano
1/4 t. pepper
1/8 t. hot pepper sauce
1 bay leaf
Garnish: shredded Cheddar
    cheese, sour cream

In a Dutch oven over medium heat, brown ground beef and onion; drain. Stir in remaining ingredients except cheese and sour cream. Bring to a boil; reduce heat and simmer for one hour. Cover; simmer for an additional 10 minutes. Discard bay leaf. Spoon into serving bowls; garnish with shredded cheese and sour cream. Makes 6 to 8 servings.

A simmering pot of chili is so easy to prepare and always welcomed by guests. Pass a basket of warm cornbread or tortilla chips, sit back and enjoy your company!

Grandpa's Favorite Chili

1-1/2 lbs. ground beef,
   browned and drained
2 15-oz. cans pinto beans
14-1/2 oz. can stewed
   tomatoes

1 onion, chopped
1 green pepper, chopped
6-oz. can tomato paste
4 T. chili powder
3 T. baking cocoa

Combine all ingredients in a large stockpot. Simmer for about one hour, until beans and vegetables are tender. Serves 6.

Sour Cream Corn Muffins

1 c. yellow cornmeal
1 c. all-purpose flour
1/4 c. sugar
2 t. baking powder
1/2 t. baking soda

1 t. salt
1 c. sour cream
2 eggs
1/4 c. butter, melted

Stir together cornmeal, flour, sugar, baking powder, baking soda and salt in a large bowl; set aside. Combine sour cream, eggs and butter in a small bowl. Mix thoroughly and add to dry ingredients; stir until moistened. Fill greased muffin cups 2/3 full. Bake at 425 degrees for 15 to 20 minutes, until golden. Makes one dozen.

Enjoy the taste of freshly made muffins any time! Freeze baked muffins in a freezer-safe bag, then just remove as many as needed and let thaw overnight in the fridge. To warm, just wrap in aluminum foil and pop into a 300-degree oven for a few minutes.

White Chicken Chili

1 onion, finely chopped
1 T. oil
4-oz. can chopped green
    chiles
2 t. garlic powder
2 t. ground cumin
2 t. dried oregano
2 t. coriander

2 t. salt
1/2 t. cayenne pepper
2 15-1/2 oz. cans Great
    Northern beans
2 10-1/2 oz. cans
    chicken broth
2 5-oz. cans chicken,
    drained

In a large stockpot over medium heat, sauté onion in oil until
tender; drain. Add chiles and seasonings; stir until well
blended. Add remaining ingredients; bring to a boil. Reduce
heat to low. Simmer for 15 to 20 minutes, until heated through.
Makes 6 to 8 servings.

It's the unexpected touches that make the biggest
impressions. When serving chili, offer guests a variety of
fun toppings...fill bowls with shredded cheese, oyster
crackers, chopped onions, sour cream and crunchy
croutons, then invite everyone to dig in!

Mexican 2-Bean Chili

3 c. cooked chicken, shredded
2 14-1/2 oz. cans chicken broth
16-oz. jar mild thick & chunky salsa
15-oz. can black beans, drained and rinsed
15-oz. can pinto beans, drained and rinsed
8-3/4 oz. can corn, drained
8-oz. can tomato sauce
1 zucchini, chopped
1 clove garlic, minced
1-1/2 to 2 t. chili powder
1 t. ground cumin
Garnish: shredded Cheddar cheese, crushed tortilla chips, sliced green onion, chopped fresh cilantro

Combine all ingredients in a large stockpot. Bring to a boil; reduce heat and simmer for 20 minutes. Ladle into bowls; top with garnishes as desired. Makes 6 servings.

Scour tag sales for big, old-fashioned enamelware stockpots. They're just the right size for family-size portions of chili and stew.

Spicy Taco Soup

1-1/2 lbs. ground beef
1 onion, chopped
1 green pepper, chopped
2 14-1/2 oz. cans diced
    tomatoes
14-1/2 oz. can tomatoes
    with chiles
16-oz. can pinto beans
    with jalapeño peppers

16-oz. can pinto beans
16-oz. can white hominy
16-oz. can yellow hominy
1-1/2 T. taco seasoning mix
1-oz. pkg. ranch salad
    dressing mix
Garnish: shredded Mexican-
    blend cheese

In a soup pot over medium heat, brown ground beef with onion
and pepper. Drain; add remaining ingredients except cheese.
Reduce heat; simmer for 30 to 45 minutes, until hot and
bubbly. Garnish with cheese. Serves 12 to 15.

Homemade savory crackers are a special touch for chili.
Spread saltines with softened butter, then sprinkle with
garlic salt, paprika or another favorite seasoning. Pop into
a 350-degree oven just until golden, 3 to 6 minutes.

Green Chile Stew with Pork

3 lbs. boneless pork loin, cubed
3 T. oil
4 c. chicken broth, divided
14-1/2 oz. can diced tomatoes
4-oz. can chopped green chiles
3 stalks celery, chopped
4 cloves garlic, minced
10-oz. jar green chile salsa
salt to taste
Optional: 11-oz. can corn, drained

Working in batches, brown pork in oil in a stockpot over medium-high heat. Remove pork and set aside, reserving drippings in stockpot; increase heat to high. Add one cup broth to reserved drippings, cooking and stirring up browned bits on bottom. When broth boils, return pork to stockpot; stir in remaining ingredients and enough of remaining broth to barely cover. Reduce heat to low; cover and simmer for 1-1/2 to 2 hours, until thickened and pork is very tender. Makes 8 servings.

Along in November, when...the skies are gray, along about five o'clock in the afternoon, I get to thinking how good chili would taste for supper. It always lives up to expectations.

-Lady Bird Johnson

3-Meat Slow-Cooker Chili

1 lb. ground beef, browned
    and drained
1 lb. ground pork sausage,
    browned and drained
1 lb. bacon, crisply cooked
    and crumbled

4 15-oz. cans tomato sauce
3 15-1/2 oz. cans kidney
    beans, drained and
    rinsed
chili seasoning to taste
15-1/4 oz. can corn, drained

Place meats in a greased slow cooker; stir in tomato sauce, beans and chili seasoning. Cover and cook on low setting for 4 to 6 hours; add corn during last hour. Serves 8.

Anything Goes Chili

1 lb. ground beef, browned
    and drained
15-1/2 oz. can kidney beans,
    drained and rinsed
14-1/2 oz. can diced
    tomatoes with garlic
    and onion

14-1/2 oz. can stewed
    tomatoes
15-1/4 oz. can corn, drained
29-oz. can tomato sauce
garlic powder to taste
2 to 3 c. cooked alphabet or
    orzo pasta

Combine all ingredients except pasta in a slow cooker. Cover and cook on low setting for 4 hours. Stir in pasta 30 minutes before serving. Makes 4 to 6 servings.

Freeze extra chili in small containers...pop in the
microwave for taco salads, chili dogs or nachos
at a moment's notice.

Jalapeño-Chicken Chili

2 c. cooked chicken, cubed
4 15-1/2 oz. cans Great
   Northern beans,
   drained and rinsed
1 onion, chopped
1/2 c. red pepper, diced
1/2 c. green pepper, diced
2 jalapeño peppers, seeded
   and finely diced

2 cloves garlic, minced
1-1/2 t. ground cumin
1/2 t. dried oregano
3/4 t. salt
1 c. water
1/2 t. chicken bouillon
   granules
1 to 2 c. salsa

Stir together all ingredients except salsa in a slow cooker. Cover and cook on low setting for 8 to 10 hours, or on high heat for 5 hours. Add salsa during last hour. Before serving, stir well to blend. Makes 6 to 8 servings.

Start tonight's dinner early and then forget about it...the handy warm setting on the slow cooker keeps chili just right for serving. Ideal for potlucks or carry-ins too!

Black Bean Chili

1 t. oil
2 onions, chopped
2 cloves garlic, minced
4-oz. can diced green chiles
2 t. chili powder
1 t. ground cumin

1 t. dried oregano
14-1/2 oz. can diced
  tomatoes
2 15-oz. cans black beans,
  drained and rinsed

Heat oil in a skillet over medium heat. Add onions and garlic; sauté until soft. Add remaining ingredients except beans. Mix well; bring to a boil. Reduce heat and simmer for 10 minutes. Stir in beans; heat through. Makes 4 to 6 servings.

To spice up familiar chili recipes, use various cheeses like smoked hot pepper or Pepper Jack. Cayenne pepper, red pepper flakes and chopped jalapeño peppers will also turn up the heat!

Garden Patch Veggie Chili

1 T. oil
3 onions, chopped
1 carrot, peeled and chopped
1 T. jalapeño pepper, chopped
4 cloves garlic, minced
3 to 4 t. chili powder
2 t. ground cumin
28-oz. can stewed tomatoes
14-oz. can stewed tomatoes
4 t. sugar
2 15-oz. cans kidney beans,
    drained and rinsed
1/3 c. bulgur wheat,
    uncooked
salt and pepper to taste

Heat oil over medium-high heat in a Dutch oven; add onions,
carrot, jalapeño, garlic and spices. Cook, stirring occasionally,
for about 5 minutes. Add tomatoes with their juice and sugar,
continue cooking about 5 minutes, stirring occasionally. Reduce
heat to low; stir in beans, bulgur wheat, salt and pepper.
Simmer until thickened, about 15 minutes. Makes 4 servings.

Need to feed a few extra guests? It's easy to stretch
chili! Some quick-cooking add-ins are canned beans,
diced tomatoes and instant rice. Simmer for just a
few minutes until heated through.

Texas Ranch Soup

1-1/2 lbs. ground beef,
   browned and drained
2 15-oz. cans ranch-style
   beans
2 14-1/2 oz. cans diced
   tomatoes

2 15-oz. cans corn
1-1/4 oz. pkg. taco
   seasoning mix
Garnish: shredded Cheddar
   cheese, crushed tortilla
   chips

Combine all ingredients except cheese and chips in a large
stockpot; bring to a boil over medium heat. Reduce heat;
simmer for 15 minutes. Spoon into bowls; garnish as desired.
Makes 6 servings.

Not enough soup bowls on hand for family & friends?
Open the cupboards and pull out sturdy mugs. They're
just as nice and the handles make them easy to hold onto.

Fiesta Skillet Cornbread

1 c. yellow cornmeal
1 c. buttermilk
2 eggs, beaten
8-oz. can creamed corn
2 jalapeño peppers, seeded
   and chopped
1 onion, chopped

3/4 t. baking soda
1/2 t. salt
1/4 c. oil
1 c. shredded Cheddar or
   Pepper Jack cheese,
   divided

Combine all ingredients except oil and cheese in a large bowl; mix well. Heat oil in a cast iron skillet; pour in half the batter. Sprinkle with half the cheese; pour remaining batter over top. Sprinkle with remaining cheese; bake at 400 degrees for 30 minutes. Cut into wedges. Makes 6 to 9 servings.

To grate or shred a block of cheese easily, place the wrapped cheese in the freezer for 10 to 20 minutes...it will just glide across the grater!

Classics

Nothing-To-It Chili

1 lb. ground beef
1 onion, chopped
15-oz. can diced tomatoes
29-oz. can hot chili beans
1-1/4 oz. pkg. chili
  seasoning mix

In a skillet over medium heat, sauté ground beef and onion together until beef is browned and onion is tender; drain. Add remaining ingredients; stir well. Simmer over low heat for 25 minutes. Makes 4 servings.

Too-Simple Tortilla Soup

3 5-oz. cans chicken
2 14-1/2 oz. cans chicken
    broth
2 15-oz. cans white hominy
16-oz. jar picante sauce
1 T. ground cumin

Combine all ingredients in a stockpot; bring to a boil. Reduce heat and warm through. Makes 6 to 8 servings.

A soup supper is warm and comforting on a cold night...so easy too. Add a loaf of bread and a fruit cobbler for dessert...done!

Corn Dollar Crisps

1 c. yellow cornmeal	2/3 c. water
1/2 t. salt	3 T. butter
1/4 t. pepper	1 t. brown sugar, packed

Mix cornmeal, salt and pepper in a medium bowl; set aside.
Combine water, butter and brown sugar in a small saucepan
over medium heat; heat until butter is melted and liquid comes
to a rolling boil. Remove from heat; pour into cornmeal mixture
and stir well. With a 1-1/4 inch cookie scoop, place mounds
on a lightly greased baking sheet. Use a glass to flatten to
1/4-inch thick. Bake at 375 degrees for 20 minutes.
Makes 4 to 6.

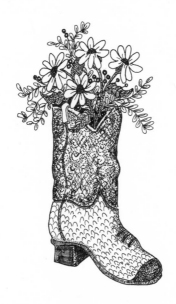

Crunchy tortilla strips are a tasty addition to
southwestern-style soups. Cut tortillas into strips, then
deep-fry quickly. Drain, then sprinkle on top of soup.

Santa Fe Chicken Chili

1/4 c. olive oil
2 lbs. boneless, skinless
   chicken breasts, cubed
4 cloves garlic, minced
4 onions, chopped
4 green peppers, diced
28-oz. can diced tomatoes
15-1/2 oz. can kidney beans,
   drained and rinsed

14-1/2 oz. can chicken broth
12-oz. jar salsa
10-oz. pkg. frozen corn
3 T. chili powder
2 t. ground cumin
1/4 t. cayenne pepper
1/2 t. salt
1/2 t. pepper

Heat oil in a large soup pot over medium heat. Sauté chicken, garlic, onions and peppers until chicken is golden and vegetables are tender. Add remaining ingredients; simmer for one hour. Makes 10 servings.

Indian Fry Bread

2 c. all-purpose flour
1-1/2 t. baking powder
1/2 t. salt

1 T. powdered milk
3/4 c. warm water
oil for deep frying

Mix together flour, baking powder, salt and milk; pour water on top. Use hands to combine; knead on a lightly floured surface until dough is smooth and elastic. Divide dough into 1-1/2 inch rounds; roll each out into a flattened circle. Heat 1/4 inch oil to 365 degrees in a skillet. Fry dough one at a time until golden, turning to fry other side. Drain on paper towels; serve warm. Makes 6 to 8 servings.

Hunting Cabin Chili

2 to 3 lbs. ground beef,
  browned and drained
28-oz. can whole tomatoes
16-oz. jar salsa
30-oz. can light red kidney
  beans, drained and
  rinsed

3 15-1/2 oz. cans dark red
  kidney beans, drained
  and rinsed
1 onion, chopped
1 green pepper, chopped
1/8 t. hot pepper sauce
salt to taste

Combine ingredients in a large soup pot. Tomato liquid should
almost cover ingredients, or a little water can be added. Bring
to a boil over medium heat; reduce heat and simmer for 2 to
3 hours. Serves 8.

A thermos of hot, delicious chili and fresh-baked
muffins wrapped up in a tea towel make a tummy-warming
present for a friend leaving on a trip
or someone working outdoors.

Fireside Chili

1-1/2 lbs. ground beef
   or pork
1 c. green pepper, chopped
1 c. onion, chopped
2 15-oz. cans kidney beans,
   drained and rinsed
28-oz. can stewed tomatoes,
   chopped
15-oz. can tomato sauce

1-1/2 c. water
2 T. Worcestershire sauce
1 T. honey
1 t. salt
2 T. chili powder
1/2 t. dried basil
1/2 t. cinnamon
1/4 t. allspice
1 bay leaf

In a Dutch oven over medium heat, cook meat, pepper and
onion until meat is browned and vegetables are tender. Drain;
stir in remaining ingredients. Reduce heat; simmer, uncovered,
for 30 minutes. Cover and simmer for one hour, stirring
occasionally. Discard bay leaf. Makes 6 to 8 servings.

There's nothing more cozy than a bowl of warm chili.
For extra comfort, warm up oven-safe bowls in
a 200-degree oven before filling...the chili,
and guests, will stay warmer longer!

Cincinnati-Style Chili

1-1/2 lbs. ground beef
2 to 3 onions, chopped
2 cloves garlic, minced
2 t. chili powder
1/4 t. cinnamon
1/8 t. nutmeg
1/8 t. ground cloves
4 c. tomato juice
2 16-oz. cans kidney beans,
    drained and rinsed

16-oz. pkg. thin spaghetti,
    cooked
1 to 2 t. butter
8-oz. pkg. shredded Cheddar
    cheese
Optional: additional chopped
    onion
Garnish: oyster crackers

In a stockpot over medium heat, brown ground beef, onions
and garlic; drain. Add spices; cook and stir for several minutes.
Stir in juice; bring to a boil. Reduce heat to low; simmer,
uncovered, for 30 minutes. Stir in beans; cover and simmer
for 15 minutes, stirring occasionally; set aside. Toss hot
spaghetti with butter. To serve, ladle chili over spaghetti. Top
with cheese for 3-way chili; add onion for 4-way. Serve with
crackers. Makes 4 to 6 servings.

Don't have a table big enough for parties? No worries!
Just make sure food you serve can be held in one hand
and eaten with a spoon or fork...chili, chips and salsa
followed by brownies or cookies are great.

Southwestern Chili Casserole

2 lbs. ground beef
1 onion, chopped
2 8-oz. cans enchilada sauce
2 15-oz. cans chili beans
    with sauce

13-1/2 oz. pkg. tortilla
    chips, divided
8-oz. pkg. shredded
    Cheddar cheese
Garnish: sour cream

Brown ground beef and onion together in a skillet over medium heat; drain. Stir in sauce and beans. Coarsely break up tortilla chips, reserving 1/2 cup for topping. Arrange remaining chips in a lightly greased 13"x9" baking pan; spread beef mixture on top. Sprinkle with reserved tortilla chips and shredded cheese. Bake, covered, at 350 degrees for 30 minutes. Remove from oven; garnish with sour cream. Serve immediately. Makes 6 servings.

Have a fiesta! After a south-of-the-border dinner, serve up some Mexican "fried" ice cream. Freeze individual scoops of ice cream while dinner's cooking, roll in crushed frosted corn flake cereal and drizzle with honey. Top with a sprinkle of cinnamon, whipped cream and a cherry.

Cheesy Turkey Rellenos

4 4-oz. cans whole green
    chiles, drained and rinsed
1/4 lb. Pepper Jack cheese,
    sliced into 1/2-inch strips
2 c. cooked turkey, sliced
    into 1/2-inch strips
1/2 c. all-purpose flour

1/2 t. baking powder
1/4 t. salt
1/2 c. milk
3 eggs
2/3 c. shredded Cheddar
    cheese

Slice chiles up one side; remove seeds and spread open flat.
Arrange in a greased 11"x7" baking pan. Fill each chile half
with strips of cheese and turkey. Fold chiles closed; place seam-
side down in pan. In a medium bowl, combine flour, baking
powder and salt. Whisk together milk and eggs; slowly add to
flour mixture, beating until smooth. Pour over chiles. Bake at
450 degrees for 15 minutes. Remove from oven and turn off
heat. Sprinkle shredded cheese over top and return to oven
until cheese is melted. Serves 6.

Tuck a jar of salsa and a bag of tortilla chips inside
a big sombrero. Add a small piñata filled with
candy...snacks and entertainment in one gift!

Chicken Tex-Mex Bake

2 12-1/2 oz. cans chicken, drained and shredded
2 10-oz. cans mild enchilada sauce
10-3/4 oz. can cream of chicken soup
4-oz. can diced green chiles
14-1/2 oz. can diced tomatoes
2-1/2 c. shredded Mexican-blend cheese, divided
1 c. sour cream
1/2 c. onion, diced
1/2 t. pepper
10 flour tortillas, cut into 1-inch squares and divided
1/2 c. sliced black olives

Combine first 5 ingredients and half of the cheese; mix well. Blend in sour cream, onion and pepper; set aside. Arrange half the tortillas in a 13"x9" baking pan sprayed with non-stick vegetable spray. Spoon a layer of chicken mixture over tortillas. Repeat layering, ending with chicken mixture on top. Sprinkle with remaining cheese; top with olives. Cover lightly with aluminum foil; bake at 350 degrees for 40 minutes, until hot and bubbly. Serves 8.

Oh-so-easy iced tea...perfect with spicy food. Fill up a
2-quart pitcher with water and drop in 6 to 8 teabags.
Refrigerate overnight. Discard teabags and add
ice cubes and sugar to taste. Cool and refreshing!

Mexican Cornbread Bake

1 lb. ground beef
1 onion, chopped
4-1/2 oz. can chopped green
   chiles, drained
1 T. chili powder

2 t. taco seasoning mix
8-oz. can Mexican-style
   tomato sauce
8-1/2 oz. pkg. cornbread mix

Brown ground beef in a skillet over medium heat; drain. Add
onion, chiles, chili powder and taco seasoning; cook until onion
is tender. Add tomato sauce; reduce heat and simmer. Prepare
cornbread mix according to package directions; pour half the
batter into a lightly greased 2-quart casserole dish. Spoon
beef mixture over batter; top with remaining batter. Bake at
350 degrees for 25 to 30 minutes, until cornbread is golden.
Serves 4 to 6.

Taking a casserole to a get-together? Wrap a pretty
bandanna around the covered baking dish and slip
the serving spoon inside the knot...keeps it right
at your fingertips!

Chili Con Queso Dip

28-oz. can plum tomatoes, drained and chopped
2 4-oz. cans chopped green chiles, drained
1 c. whipping cream
16-oz. pkg. shredded Cheddar cheese
salt and pepper to taste

Combine tomatoes and chiles in a medium saucepan over low heat. Simmer for about 15 minutes. Stirring constantly, add cream and cheese; continue cooking until mixture thickens. Add salt and pepper to taste; serve warm. Makes 6 cups.

Make your own tortilla chips to go with homemade dips and salsas...you won't believe how easy it is! Just slice flour tortillas into wedges, spray with non-stick vegetable spray and bake at 350 degrees for 5 to 7 minutes.

Oh-So-Cheesy Chili Dip

8-oz. pkg. cream cheese
15-oz. can chili

8-oz. pkg. shredded Cheddar
cheese

Place cream cheese in a 9" glass pie plate. Soften in microwave on high setting for one minute; spread in pie plate. Spoon chili over cream cheese; top with shredded cheese. Microwave on high setting for 4 to 6 minutes, or until cheese is hot and bubbly. Serve warm. Makes about 4 cups.

Spicy Tex-Mex Party Mix

2-1/2 c. lightly salted
    peanuts
2-1/2 c. lightly salted
    pretzels
3 c. corn chips

3 c. shredded wheat cereal
1-1/4 oz. pkg. taco
    seasoning mix
1/4 c. butter, melted

Combine all ingredients in a large bowl; toss well to coat. Store in an airtight container. Makes 11 cups.

Taking a good mouthful, I felt as though I had taken liquid fire...the tomato was chile colorado, or red pepper, of the purest kind.

–William T. Sherman

Chili Dog Sauce

1 lb. ground beef
2 c. water
1 T. onion, diced
1 T. paprika
2 t. chili powder
2 t. ground cumin

1 t. dried oregano
1/4 to 1/2 t. red pepper
   flakes
1/4 t. pepper
1/8 t. ground cloves

Brown ground beef in a skillet; drain. Stir in remaining ingredients; cover and simmer over medium-low heat until liquid has reduced to sauce consistency. Makes enough sauce for 6 to 12 hot dogs.

Clever condiments! When serving Mexican meals, slice the tops off green peppers, rinse and remove seeds. Then fill with guacamole, sour cream and salsa. Cover with reserved tops and refrigerate until ready to serve.

Chili Burger Mix

1 T. all-purpose flour	2 T. dried, minced onion
1-1/2 t. chili powder	1 t. seasoned salt
1/2 t. red pepper flakes	1/2 t. dried, minced garlic
1/2 t. sugar	1/2 t. ground cumin

Combine all ingredients, store in an airtight container in a cool, dry place for up to 6 months. Attach instructions. Makes about 1/4 cup.

Instructions:

Combine one to 1-1/2 tablespoons seasoning mix with one pound ground beef. Mix well and form into patties; grill to desired doneness. Makes 4.

Create a warm glow using box graters picked up at flea markets. The more character, the better, so look for ones that have darkened with age and are even a bit worn. Simply tuck a votive or tealight inside...so simple!

Mexican Bean Soup in a Jar

3/4 c. dried pinto beans
3/4 c. dried kidney beans
6 cubes chicken bouillon
2 T. dried, minced onion
2 T. dried parsley
1 T. chili powder

2 t. ground cumin
1 t. dried oregano
1/2 c. long-cooking rice, uncooked
1 c. wagon wheel pasta, uncooked

Layer beans in a one-quart, wide-mouth jar. Combine bouillon cubes and seasonings in a small plastic sandwich bag; seal. Place rice and pasta in separate sandwich bags; seal. Tuck bags into quart jar for gift giving; attach instructions.

Instructions:

Remove packets from jar; set aside. Place beans in a large stockpot with 4 cups water. Bring to a boil; cover and remove from heat. Let stand for one hour; drain beans and return to stockpot. Add 8 cups water and contents of seasoning packet. Bring to a boil; reduce heat, cover and simmer for one hour, or until beans are tender. Stir in rice; bring to a simmer. Cover and simmer for 15 minutes. Uncover; stir in pasta and 1/2 cup water. Simmer for 10 minutes, or until pasta is tender. Makes 8 to 10 servings.

Give Mexican Bean Soup in a Jar with homemade salsa and a bag of chips to snack on while the chili is cooking.

Cowboy Cornbread Mix

1 c. yellow cornmeal	1 T. baking powder
1 c. all-purpose flour	1 t. baking soda
1/4 c. sugar	1/8 t. salt

Combine all ingredients; mix well and place in an airtight container. Attach instructions.

Instructions:

Place cornbread mix in a large bowl; set aside. Whisk together 3 tablespoons melted, cooled butter and 1-1/3 cups buttermilk in a separate bowl; add in one egg. Pour into cornbread mix; stir just until combined. Spread in a greased 8"x8" baking pan. Bake at 425 degrees for 30 minutes. Makes 6 servings.

Pack the cornbread mix into a gift bag for a much-appreciated hostess surprise! Cut 2 back pockets from a pair of old blue jeans, arrange on the front of a white gift bag and secure with hot glue. Slip a sassy red bandanna in one pocket and a gift card in the other.

Host a Chili Cook-off!

You're invited to a Chili Cook-off!

Where: _____

When: _____

RSVP: _____

_____

Bring: _____

1ˢᵗ Place

_____

_____

Make copies of these little tags for the winners!
(Spiciest, Most Original, etc.)

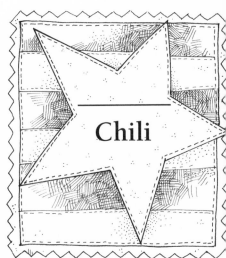

_____

Chili

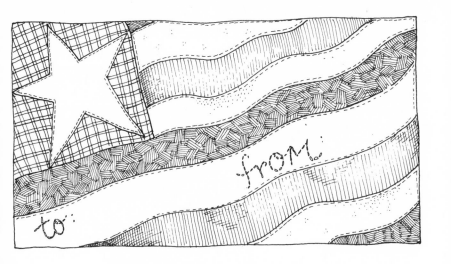

Gift Mix Tags!

Just copy these tags, color with markers
& tie 'em on. So easy!

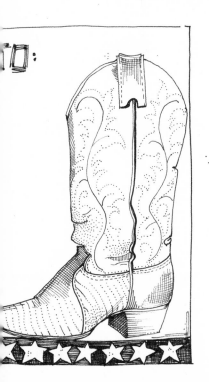

Index